The Library of
Future Weather and Climate

Floods
of the Future

Paul Stein

The Rosen Publishing Group, Inc.
New York

Published in 2001 by The Rosen Publishing Group, Inc.
29 East 21st Street, New York, NY 10010

Copyright © 2001 by The Rosen Publishing Group, Inc.

First Edition

Library of Congress Cataloging-in-Publication Data
Stein, Paul, 1968–
Floods of the future / Paul Stein. — 1st ed.
p. cm. — (The library of future weather and climate)
Includes bibliographical references and index.
ISBN 0-8239-3412-8 (lib. bdg.)
1. Floods—Juvenile literature. 2. Sea level—Juvenile literature. 3.
Climatic changes—Environmental aspects—Juvenile literature.
[1.Floods. 2. Climatic changes. 3. Nature—Effect of human beings on.]
I. Title.
GB1399 .S72 2001
551.48'9—dc21

0100-58060-mm

00-012139

All temperatures in this book are in degrees Fahrenheit, except where
specifically noted. To convert to degrees Celsius, or centigrade, use the
following formula:

Celsius temperature = (5 ÷ 9) x (the temperature in Fahrenheit - 32)

Manufactured in the United States of America

Contents

Introduction

The summer of 1999 had been a dry one for the New York City area. Months of below-average rainfall had withered lawns and strained water supplies. In the suburbs outside of the city, streams and wells ran dry. Day after day of blazing heat and humidity added to the misery. The millions of residents who lived in and around the city, including those on Long Island and in New Jersey, looked forward to rain and relief from the drought that had lasted so long.

When the rains returned, however, they came with a vengeance. It was as if all the rain that had been withheld through the summer finally came down all at once. The first flood came on August 11 in Suffolk County, Long Island, a densely populated suburb of New York City. From Deer Park to

Manorville, slow-moving thunderstorms soaked the region with as much as five inches of rain. Water poured down from the sky at the rate of two inches per hour in some locations. Many roads were closed as up to four feet of water carried away cars, some with people still inside. Fortunately, however, nobody was injured. And hours after the storms hit, the water receded from the roads, leaving only puddles.

Just a little more than two weeks later, however, the weather repeated itself. And this time, the results were more damaging. Drenching thunderstorms, fed by humid, southerly winds, moved slowly over the heart of New York City during the morning rush hour. As much as five inches of rain came down in three hours, "like a waterfall" according to one eyewitness, and overwhelmed the city's drainage system. Roads quickly flooded, with emergency officials rescuing people from eighty cars on one highway alone. Water cascaded into the New York City subways, flooding some tracks to a depth of four feet and shutting down subway service across most of Manhattan. Some subway tunnels turned into raging rivers. And above ground in the Bronx, a borough of New York City, torrential rains submerged a section of tracks used by dozens of trains carrying tens of thousands of commuters in from the suburbs. One train carrying around 800 people was trapped for over six hours by the flood. Dozens of other trains never made it into the city. In just a few hours, the unexpected downpour had crippled New York City's transportation system, disrupting the

In September 1999, Hurricane Floyd devastated the coastal regions of North Carolina and Virginia, and caused six deaths and hundreds of injuries when it spawned flash floods in New Jersey.

lives of thousands of people. Most residents had never seen anything like it. But the worst was yet to come.

Just three weeks later, in the early morning hours of September 16, Hurricane Floyd barreled inland across the coast of North Carolina with winds gusting to over 100 miles per hour. Once inland, Floyd lost most of its wind energy and was downgraded to tropical storm status. But by no means had it lost its destructive potential. Floyd churned northward across North Carolina and Virginia that day, and by late in the day, the leading edge of the tropical rains had spread across New Jersey. As the remains of Floyd moved over the state during the next twenty-four hours, New

Storm–induced flooding can threaten entire communities.

Jersey suffered its worst weather-related disaster in history. The saturated, tropical air carried by Floyd unleashed torrents of rain. Five to ten inches were common, with some spots recording over a foot—the same amount that normally falls over three months' time. Rivers and streams overflowed, some swelling to levels never before recorded, flooding town after town. Six people died in the floods, and over 100 were injured. Tens of thousands of homes and businesses were damaged or destroyed, and over 600,000 people lost power, some for up to a week. Damage was tallied at over $1 billion in New Jersey alone. Farther south, Floyd caused even worse flooding in North Carolina, where more than fifty people died.

The flooding in the New York City region during the late summer of 1999 was indeed extraordinary. But floods have always occurred throughout history, from Biblical times to the present day. Tragic and destructive though they may be, floods are naturally occurring events, related to processes that occur in the earth's atmosphere. In the future, we can expect more floods to wash over our landscapes from time to time in various parts of the world, just as they have done in the past.

But there's more. In recent years, scientists have become increasingly concerned about a warming of the earth's climate. This "global warming" has accelerated in the last part of the twentieth century, and many scientists think it is caused at least in part by our continuing release of carbon dioxide and other gases into the earth's atmosphere. If the trend persists, as many expect, global warming may have profound consequences for the earth's climate in the decades to come. What effect might global warming have on floods of the future? In order to examine this question, this book first considers the natural cycle of water on our planet. Then it discusses floods, how they happen, and how they might be affected by climate change. Though there's no evidence that global warming contributed to the cloudbursts in the New York City region in the late summer of 1999, these events serve as examples of the kind of flooding that may become more frequent in the future.

1 Water on Our Planet

Mount Waialeale, on the island of Kauai, Hawaii, is not a place you would want to visit for a sunny, tropical vacation. An astonishing 460 inches—over thirty-eight feet—of rain drenches the mountain each year, on average. The cloud-shrouded peak is a continuous cascade of waterfalls and gushing rivers that tumble back into the ocean.

On the other hand, Arica, Chile, is not a place where you would want to grow a garden. A mere 0.03 inches of rain sprinkles down each year, on average. The weather in this harbor town, located on the Pacific coast of northern Chile, is a nearly unbroken string of sunny days and clear, starry nights. It would take Arica 15,000 years to accumulate the amount of rain that falls in one year on Mount Waialeale.

A fishing fleet seeks its daily catch in the early morning fog. Fog, like clouds, is composed of tiny droplets of water.

In the mountains of Kauai, Hawaii, an inch of rain is a daily occurrence. Through centuries of storms, the Hawaiian mountains have adapted to handle hundreds of inches of rain per year. The landscape around Arica, Chile, is accustomed to only sprinklings. In Arica, even an inch of rain would be enough to cause a flood. Geography has much to do with flooding. But first you have to have a lot of rain, relative to the amount that normally falls in a given location. What determines how much rain falls in different locations around the world?

We must first consider the nature of water on our planet. Water can exist in three different forms, or "phases." These phases include solid ice, liquid water, and invisible, gaseous water vapor. Depending on the temperature and other factors, water can easily change from one phase to another. This chameleon-like ability of water allows it to continuously circulate between the surface of the earth and the sky. This cycle of water is known to scientists as the hydrologic cycle.

One place to start describing the hydrologic cycle is with the processes of evaporation and condensation. Evaporation is the process by which liquid water changes into gaseous water vapor. It happens when an energized water molecule breaks free from the surface of liquid water and floats off into the atmosphere. We see evaporation at work when we watch a plume of steam rising off a boiling pot of water and vanishing in the air. But evaporation isn't a process that requires boiling water. It occurs constantly from the surfaces of puddles, rivers, oceans, and any other body of water on the planet.

The process of condensation is the opposite of evaporation. Condensation occurs when invisible, gaseous water vapor turns back into liquid water. This can happen when water vapor molecules collide with a body of water, such as a river or ocean. Or it can happen when individual water vapor molecules collide in the air and stick to one another or to other tiny floating objects such as airborne dust or salt particles from the sea. We've all seen the process of condensation in the bathroom, when the mirror fogs over during a hot shower.

Condensation and evaporation are always occurring at the same time throughout the atmosphere. Water vapor molecules are constantly colliding with one another and briefly condensing into tiny liquid water droplets before breaking apart again and evaporating.

Rates of evaporation depend on the temperature and humidity of the air.

And on the surface of a body of water, molecules are constantly flying back and forth between the water and the air, liquid changing into water vapor and vice versa on a microscopic level. What's important is which process is occurring faster.

There are two important factors that influence how fast evaporation and condensation occur. The first is temperature. In general, the higher the temperature, the faster the water molecules move around and the more easily they can fly apart and evaporate. Likewise, the lower the temperature, the slower the molecules move and the more likely they are to stick together and condense when they collide with one another, or with other objects. The second important influence on the rates of condensation and evaporation is the humidity of the air. The higher the humidity, the higher the water vapor content and the more collisions there are between water vapor molecules. The more collisions, the more frequently condensation will occur. Other factors that play a role in condensation and evaporation include the size and shape of the body of water (whether it's a flat surface, like the surface of a lake, or curved, like a raindrop). Also, foreign molecules mixed in with liquid water affect its ability to evaporate.

And so we begin the hydrologic cycle, with the evaporation of water from the surface of the earth. From lakes, oceans, and other bodies of water, water vapor molecules break free from their liquid bonds and drift away by the millions into the sky. At the same time, plants and trees are constantly giving off some of their stored water through tiny pores on the undersides of their leaves in a process called transpiration. Whatever the source, water vapor rises through the atmosphere and is blown around the world by the wind. There's always some water vapor in the air, even on the driest days and in the middle of the largest deserts. The more humid the air is, the more water vapor it contains.

Plants release stored water into the atmosphere through tiny pores—a process called transpiration.

In the next part of the hydrologic cycle, clouds play a major role. Clouds develop when rising air carries water vapor high into the sky. When air rises, it moves into regions of lower air pressure because there are fewer air molecules weighing down from above. Moving into an area of lower pressure, the air is able to expand and become less dense. Air molecules (including water vapor) therefore move around more slowly on average, and the air cools. As the air gets colder, the water molecules will collide and condense more frequently than they will fly apart and evaporate. When the rate of condensation exceeds the rate of evaporation, tiny liquid water droplets form by the millions, causing a cloud to appear.

Since clouds form high in the sky, where the air is much colder than it is at the surface of the earth, most clouds contain a mixture of water droplets and ice crystals. The more water vapor there is in the air and the higher the air rises, the larger the cloud grows. Water droplets and ice crystals become larger as more water vapor condenses from the air. They also grow by colliding with one another and merging together. If these cloud particles are able to grow large enough, the force of gravity takes over and they fall to the ground as snow or rain. Scientists use the term "precipitation" to describe snow, rain, or anything else that forms inside a cloud and falls to the ground. Precipitation is the third part of the hydrologic cycle.

Whether precipitation falls from a thunderstorm or a snowstorm, the next step in the hydrologic cycle is runoff. Runoff is the process by which water on land is pulled by gravity from higher elevations to

Clouds are formed when the rate of condensation exceeds the rate of evaporation, resulting in millions of water particles gathering in the sky.

lower elevations and eventually into the oceans. A drenching rain-storm causes water to run off down streets and into the sewer, or directly into larger streams and rivers. Or the rainwater just soaks into the ground, some of it percolating down into large under-ground reservoirs, and some drawn upward into plants. During colder weather, snow collects on the ground and melts in the spring, running off or soaking into the soil just like rain.

And so we return to where we began, with evaporation. While evaporation removes water from the surface of the earth and adds it to the atmosphere, rain, snow, and runoff remove water from the atmos-phere and replenish the earth. Across the earth, the total amount of water in the hydrologic cycle remains nearly the same. However, in dif-ferent places, different parts of the hydrologic cycle are more important. These differences are driven largely by the local climate, which in turn is influ-enced by a variety of factors. For example, the sunny, dry weather of Arica, Chile, is dom-inated by evaporation. This is because the atmosphere over Arica is very stable most of the time. A stable atmosphere is one in which air does not easily

Runoff occurs when gravity pulls water from higher elevations to lower areas.

rise. Remember that clouds are produced by rising air, so when air doesn't rise, clouds don't form and rain is scarce. Another reason that Arica's climate is so dry and stable is because the nearby ocean water is so cold. The ocean water cools the air above it, causing it to become denser and to resist upward air currents.

In the mountains of Kauai, however, condensation is the driving force in the local weather (though without evaporation from the nearby ocean, Kauai would be much less wet). The atmosphere over Kauai is very unstable, and rising air results in frequent cloudiness and rainfall. In contrast to northern Chile, the ocean water around Kauai is relatively warm. This warms the air above, causing it to become less dense and expand as the molecules move around faster. As air expands and becomes less dense, it rises, carrying tropical moisture high into the sky. The mountains of Kauai cause the air to rise even faster. Wind blowing into the sides of the steep mountains is forced upward, pumping more and more moisture into the atmosphere. In effect, the Kauai mountains are a cloud factory that produces rain in torrential amounts.

In addition to varying in different parts of the world, the hydrologic cycle also varies over time. Once in a while, many days or even weeks go by without rain or snow. If the dry weather persists long enough, a drought occurs. Sometimes, on the other hand, rain or snow fall much faster and heavier than usual, soaking the ground with far more water than it is accustomed to handling. When this happens, a flood occurs. In the next chapter we discuss different kinds of floods and the weather that spawns them.

2 When Water Rises

In the evening of June 14, 1990, lightning began to flicker in the humid, cloud-filled sky over southeastern Ohio. Rumbles of thunder echoed off the rolling, forested hills. It had been a wet spring in Shadyside, a quiet community of 3,900 people nestled along the gently curving banks of the Ohio River. In fact, nearly twice the normal amount of rain had fallen during May, and the wet conditions had continued into the early part of June. But thunderstorms are a normal part of the spring and summertime weather in this part of the country. Local residents had no reason to expect it would be anything other than just another rainy June evening.

Flash floods are especially destructive when torrential rains fall on ground already saturated with water.

As darkness descended on Shadyside that night, however, the full force of the thunderstorm began to pour down from above. As though a giant faucet in the sky had suddenly opened, a month's worth of rain burst from the clouds in just an hour and fifteen minutes. With the ground already soaked from weeks of heavy rain, none of the thunderstorm's rainfall was absorbed into the earth. Instead, it rushed in sheets down the waterlogged hills and into the valleys. Two small streams, the Pipe and Wegee Creeks, were closest to the cloudburst and suffered the greatest share of the cascade. A surge of water, mud, and rocks as high as thirty feet raced down the normally tranquil creeks, smashing houses and washing away cars. Roads were torn up. Trees were toppled. Some people scrambled out of their houses and up the hills to safety. Others were not as lucky. By 10 PM, the leading edge of the flood plunged into the Ohio River, carrying the splintered remains of buildings, crumpled vehicles, and many of the twenty-six victims of the raging water. Two bodies were later found about thirty miles downstream.

The disaster at Shadyside, Ohio, in June of 1990 is an example of a kind of flood known as a flash flood, so named because of its speed. Flash floods most often happen when a strong thunderstorm moves slowly over an area, dumping extremely heavy rain in a short period of time. Flash floods can also happen when several thunderstorms line up and move over the same location, one behind the other. As with Shadyside, if the ground is already waterlogged from above-average rainfall, the effects of heavy thunderstorms will be much worse.

In the case of Shadyside, violent surges of water came crashing down two normally quiet streams in a matter of minutes. Other floods, no less destructive, can take days to engulf the land. In a river flood, the water level may rise at the rate of only a few inches every twenty-four hours. River floods occur for different reasons than flash floods. Owing to their small size and shallow depth, streams and creeks can flood quickly from thunderstorm rains. Rivers, on the other hand, are much deeper and wider, and require much more rain over a longer period of time to flood. Sometimes, well-above normal rainfall over a period of weeks or months can cause a river to over-flow its banks. At other times, a river will overflow as a result of torrential rains from a hurricane or tropical storm that has moved inland. But rain isn't the only cause of river flooding.

A devastating river flood occurred along the Red River in North Dakota and western Minnesota in the spring of 1997 as a result of melt-ing snow. That winter had been a particularly harsh one in the northern Plains, following an unusually wet late autumn in 1996. Blizzards struck

River floods can occur if too much meltwater from snow overwhelms the normal waterways of an area, such as when the Red River rose to twenty-two feet above normal in April 1997.

North and South Dakota and western Minnesota with unusual ferocity and frequency, piling up snow by the foot. By the end of the winter, some locations had gotten over 100 inches of snow—two to three times the normal amount. A final snowstorm in early April dumped another foot of snow on the region, setting the stage for disaster.

Flooding came as the snow began to melt. Normally, the winter snowpack dissolves slowly over months under warming spring sunshine. This releases meltwater gradually, preventing significant flooding. In the spring of 1997, however, cold air kept most of the record snowpack locked in place. When the winter snowpack finally melted after the final April storm, too much water was let loose across the land too fast. Large sections of the countryside were transformed into a vast lake. Over a period of weeks, the Red River, which flows northward into Canada along the border of North Dakota and Minnesota, swelled to unprecedented heights from the enormous amount of meltwater. In Fargo, North Dakota, the river crested at over twenty-two feet above normal on April 17. The worst hit towns, however, were Grand Forks, North Dakota, and East Grand Forks, Minnesota. There, the Red River surged to twenty-six feet above flood stage, putting 90 percent of East Grand Forks under water and forcing the evacuation of 60,000 people. The frigid water flowed through buildings and into houses. Cars bobbed up and down among jagged chunks of floating ice. The final insult occurred as flood waters prevented firefighters from reaching a blaze that swept through eleven buildings in the heart of the downtown area. In all, flood damage totaled close to $4 billion.

Cars were submerged along with 90 percent of the town when East Grand Forks, Minnesota, was hit by a flood.

Surprisingly, a third type of flood has nothing to do with heavy rain or melting snow. Storm surge flooding happens when strong winds push ocean water inland, flooding low-lying coastal areas. Wind speeds must be unusually high and last for hours at a time to accomplish this feat. These kinds of conditions are found only in the strongest of storm systems. Storm surge flooding from hurricanes, for example, can be particularly devastating. Depending on the strength of the winds, hurricanes can drive ocean water levels to twenty feet or more above normal. Pounding waves add to the damage. Many coastal communities are especially vulnerable to storm surge flooding since they are built on thin, long islands only several feet above the ocean surface.

Storm surge can also happen when strong wintertime storm systems, sometimes 1,000 miles in diameter, track slowly along coastal regions. These storm systems, often called nor'easters along the Atlantic seaboard of the United States, can produce winds of hurricane force (seventy-four miles per hour) or higher. An especially destructive example of storm surge flooding occurred during an extraordinarily powerful winter storm in March 1993.

The storm surge was unusual in that it occurred along the Gulf Coast of Florida, a region where surge from winter storms was not considered a threat. Nor'easters almost always form far away from Florida, well to the north along the coasts of North Carolina, Virginia, or Maryland. But on March 13, 1993, a winter storm as powerful as a hurricane formed over the northern Gulf of Mexico, west of Florida. Strong southerly winds ahead of the storm pulled ocean water northward along the western coast of Florida. There it piled up in Apalachee Bay, a broad curve in the northwestern Florida coastline where the waters of the Gulf of Mexico are especially shallow. As the rapidly strengthening storm system moved inland from the Gulf of Mexico

This satellite photo shows Hurricane Floyd moving just off the coast of Florida on September 14, 1999. Hurricanes can cause very destructive flooding from storm surges.

across the southeastern United States, the winds along the Florida coastline suddenly shifted. Gusting out of the west at over seventy miles per hour, the howling gales pushed inland all the excess ocean water that had piled up in Apalachee Bay. It was 4:30 in the morning, still dark, when the homes of unsuspecting residents in Taylor County, Florida, starting filling with cold, churning sea water. Outside their windows, the ocean had overtaken the land. The surging ocean rose as high as twelve feet above normal. Seven people drowned.

The earth's atmosphere is constantly changing. Floods are often random events, caused by periods of unusually wet or stormy weather that naturally occur every once in a while. But sometimes there's an

Coastal storms wrought destruction in Malibu, California, in June 1998. Dirt and debris, along with the remains of a backyard deck, litter the hillside.

unseen driving force behind the heavy rain or snow: the temperature of the oceans. El Niño, the warming of ocean water in the tropical eastern Pacific, and La Niña, the cooling of ocean water in the same area, have been linked to flooding events in certain parts of the world.

When ocean temperatures in the tropical eastern Pacific rise well above normal, as in a strong El Niño event, major changes occur in the atmosphere. El Niño adds energy, in the form of heat and moisture, to the air overhead. This causes weather patterns to shift over the tropical eastern Pacific. When weather patterns change over such a large area, it often has a ripple effect around the world. Scientists link strong El Niño events to a likelihood of flooding in Ecuador and Peru, as well as across the southern United States. A strong La Niña event, on the other hand, is known for producing floods in northern Australia and Southeast Asia. When scientists see a major El Niño or La Niña event on the horizon, therefore, certain parts of the world go on the alert for wet and stormy weather.

Flash floods, river floods, and storm surge are different kinds of floods that occur in different situations. Whether the cause is heavy rain from thunderstorms, too much water from melting snow, or high winds pushing the ocean inland, floods are products of the weather. Many scientists have recently become alarmed by signs that global weather conditions are changing. In the next chapter we explore global warming, a phenomenon that may have profound consequences for weather-related events such as floods.

3 Our Warming Planet

Fort Collins, Colorado, July 1997. A flash flood spawned by tropical-like rainfall sweeps down normally placid Spring Creek, killing five and causing $190 million in damage.

Eastern Spain, August 1996. Flood waters race out of the Pyrenees and through a campground filled with vacationers, killing over sixty people.

Wad-Sulayman Valley in the Sudan, Africa, October 1998. Sixty-three members of an unsuspecting nomadic tribe camping in a valley are swept to their deaths by a flash flood.

Hunan Province, China, August 1999. A foot of rain in one day leads to flooding that kills seventy-seven and forces 120,000 from their homes.

Venezuela, December 1999. Flash floods and mudslides pour down the mountainsides and through coastal cities following intense rainstorms. Tens of thousands are killed and hundreds of thousands are left homeless.

Around the world, sometimes it seems like the weather is running amuck. On the TV news, we see images of raging, muddy waters pouring through the narrow streets of a small town in Europe. Or we see shots looking down from a helicopter at hundreds of houses destroyed by mudslides in South America. Or we see dramatic scenes of people being rescued from a raging river in the United States.

As we've discussed, floods have always occurred on our planet. The atmosphere is sometimes stormy, sometimes quiet. Weather extremes, such as the torrential cloudbursts that produce flooding, are a normal part of the earth's climate. But are those extremes getting more frequent?

Some scientists think so; others do not. One study published in 1997 by a scientist at the National Climatic Data Center stated that the number of extreme rain events in the United States had increased by 20 percent since 1900. Critics of the study pointed to the fact that the excess rainfall events amounted to only one additional day every two years, which is within the limits of what could be expected in the natural swings of the weather. The scientist who authored the study countered by saying that the increase in heavy rain has only a 5 to 10 percent chance of being due to natural variations in the weather.

One thing that is not in question, however, is the rise in global temperatures. Our planet is getting warmer. The year 1999 was the twenty-first consecutive year in which the global mean temperature was above the long-term average. The ten warmest years in recorded history, dating back nearly a century and a half, have all occurred since the early 1980s. The 1990s were the warmest decade in recorded history, with 1998 being the warmest year of them all. And by reconstructing global temperature trends over the last thousand years, researchers are able to state that in all likelihood, the 1990s were the warmest decade of the millennium.

Climatologists know, however, that warm and cold spells lasting thousands of years have come and gone throughout history. For example, ice ages have frozen large parts of the earth numerous times in the distant past. The most recent ice age peaked around 20,000 years ago, when the average global temperature was five to nine degrees lower than it is today. Life on earth was very different back then, as glaciers expanded to cover large parts of North America, northern Europe, and Asia.

By contrast, there have also been periods of warm global weather, when snow and ice became confined to the poles and winterlike weather was largely unknown. For example, the Cretaceous period, between 145 and 65 million years ago, was characterized by a warm, greenhouse-like environment. This was the age of the dinosaurs, when tropical plants and animals thrived as far north as the northern parts of modern-day Canada.

These kinds of drastic changes in climate are caused by a variety of natural processes. Scientists look to the Sun as one of the primary

In October 1996, following a volcanic eruption, a break appeared under the Vatnajokull glacier, which covers 10 percent of Iceland. This caused heavy floods in the southeastern part of the country.

sources for climate change. The Sun heats the earth and drives the earth's weather machine. It's logical that if the energy output of the Sun changes, then the amount of energy received by the earth—and therefore its temperature—should change. In fact, scientists do observe a fairly regular, eleven-year solar cycle in which the energy output of the Sun rises and falls. Other changes in the amount of energy emitted from the Sun can occur more irregularly, adding further unpredictability to climate change.

Another mechanism linked to the swings of climate over long periods of time is the slowly changing orbit of the earth. The path that the earth takes around the Sun changes slowly over tens of thousands of years, as does the tilt of the earth on its axis. The total effect of these orbital changes is to alter the way that solar energy is distributed between high latitudes on the earth, near the poles, and low latitudes closer to the equator. Changing the distribution of energy like this causes changes in weather and climate.

Other events that can alter climate include volcanoes, which spew haze-forming gases into the atmosphere. If the eruption is big enough, the haze can circle the globe and block a small amount of incoming sunlight, resulting in a slight global cooling. Or consider the oceans, which exert a major influence on climate. Long, slow-moving currents, such as the Gulf Stream, carry warm and cold water around the planet. In so doing they warm or cool the air above them. Sometimes these currents can shift, or break down, leading to surprisingly rapid changes in climate.

Humans, however, have attracted the most attention as a cause for the recent global warming trend. It became clear in the last half of the twentieth century that the burning of fossil fuels may be having an effect on the average global temperature. Fossil fuels include coal, natural gas, and oil. They're so-named because they are created deep underground over millions of years from the fossilized remains of plants. Plants, like all life, are based on carbon molecules. When people burn fossil fuels to make energy, they release this carbon into the atmosphere in the form of gaseous carbon dioxide.

Since the late 1950s, the amount of carbon dioxide in the earth's atmosphere has risen 30 percent. Scientists think that this trend actually began some 300 years ago, at the start of the Industrial Revolution. This was the time when humans first discovered the energy-giving property of coal. Oil and natural gas followed in the centuries to come, as fossil fuels quickly became the primary source of energy worldwide. Today, most modern conveniences rely on the burning of fossil fuels. Not only machines with engines, like cars and planes, but anything that uses electricity. The majority of our electricity is generated by power plants that burn fossil fuels for power.

Carbon dioxide has a profound effect on the earth's climate. It is called a greenhouse gas because it efficiently absorbs a kind of energy known as radiation. Radiation consists of invisible electromagnetic waves that travel at the speed of light. Everything both gives off and absorbs radiation, and the amount of radiation coming into and going out of an object determines the object's temperature. If an object

Climate depends on a wide variety of factors. Erupting volcanoes, for example, throw gases into the atmosphere that can block sunlight and cause slight variations in the earth's temperature.

Carbon dioxide and other, more dangerous greenhouse gases are spewed into the atmosphere by factories that typically consume fossil fuel to produce energy and manufacture products.

absorbs more radiation than it receives, it warms. If it gives off more radiation than it absorbs, it cools. The temperature of the earth is linked to the exchange of radiation between the Sun, the surface of the earth, and the earth's atmosphere.

Carbon dioxide and other greenhouse gases, such as methane, water vapor, and chlorofluorocarbons, warm the atmosphere by absorbing radiation given off by the earth. This warming process is known as the greenhouse effect. It's a natural process, without which life could not exist on the planet. Without the greenhouse effect, the average temperature of the earth would be well below freezing. With the greenhouse effect, our average temperature is close to 60°F.

The problem occurs as humans add more and more greenhouse gases to the atmosphere through the burning of fossil fuels. The more of these gas molecules there are in the air, the more energy is absorbed and the warmer the atmosphere becomes. Scientists estimate that the average temperature of the earth was about 1°F warmer at the end of the twentieth century than at the beginning. Computer simulations of climate project a further global warming of two to six degrees over the twenty-first century. If this forecast comes true, it would represent the biggest change in our planet's climate in thousands of years.

Much uncertainty remains, however, since the climate change observed so far isn't quite enough to distinguish it from the climate change that occurs naturally over time. Also, our understanding of the earth's climate in all its complexity remains incomplete.

Scientists debate the role of clouds and water vapor in the air, and how they might serve to enhance or dissipate the warming trend. And we don't yet know exactly how the atmosphere interacts with the oceans, though we do know that their relationship is extremely important.

The greenhouse effect occurs when gases such as carbon dioxide or methane trap energy from the earth's radiation in the atmosphere, thereby warming the planet.

Despite all this, more and more scientists are becoming convinced that global warming is at least partially the result of the increasing amount of greenhouse gases in the atmosphere. The consequences of this rise in temperature are most noticeable in the colder parts of the world. Many glaciers throughout the world are shrinking as they melt away in the warmer air. Vast sheets of ice in Antarctica are breaking apart at an accelerating rate. Polar ice is crumbling.

While it's unclear whether global warming has contributed to any recent flooding events around the world, scientists do know that changing climate may have an effect on the hydrologic cycle. And since precipitation is a key process in the hydrologic cycle, there may be a link between global warming and flooding. In the next chapter we examine what that link might be.

4 Future Floods

The connection between global warming and flooding is not obvious. It's easy to see how global warming might result in milder winters with less snow and hotter summers with prolonged heat waves. Scientists think that droughts may become more severe and last longer in some parts of the world if the current global warming trend continues. Surprisingly, however, global warming may not only result in too little rain in some parts of the world, but too much rain in other parts. Drought and flooding, the opposite extremes of the hydrologic cycle, may both become more severe in the decades to come.

Scientists theorize that global warming may contribute to more severe weather conditions in the next few decades, which may mean more extreme cases of flooding and drought.

The reason for such an energized hydrologic cycle has to do with evaporation rates. Recall that the rate of evaporation is affected by the amount of water vapor already in the air, the wind speed, and the amount of sunshine. Most important, evaporation rates generally increase as temperatures increase. In a warmer world decades from now, countless millions of additional water molecules will be flying off the surfaces of oceans, lakes, and rivers.

Obviously this may cause droughts to become more severe and last longer than they do today. A higher evaporation rate in a warmer world would cause the ground to lose moisture faster. In certain kinds of weather patterns, rising temperatures in upper levels of the atmosphere may cause the air to become more stable. Air is said to be stable when it does not easily rise. Since clouds and rain need rising air to form, a warmer, more stable atmosphere over a particular region would result in drier weather. Wouldn't this tend to lessen the amount of flooding in the future?

Certainly flooding would be much less likely to occur in a region suffering from drought. But drought conditions would not be occurring everywhere, only in certain parts of the world. Droughts are caused by weather patterns that deflect rain-bearing weather systems away from an area for an extended period of time. Lack of clouds and rain allows sunshine, hot air, and evaporation to dry out the land. The same weather pattern that forces storm systems away from one area, however, may direct them over another area. It's often the case that while one part of the country suffers from drought,

Scientists can use computer simulations called climate models to predict future atmospheric weather patterns.

another is getting above-average rainfall. And where the rain falls, it may be heavier in the future because higher evaporation rates have added more water vapor to the air.

Computers have helped to verify this possibility. Scientists use supercomputers to run complex simulations of the climate of the future. They program the computer to predict how the atmosphere will behave if carbon dioxide amounts are doubled. These simulations, called climate models, are the most advanced tools scientists have for predicting how global warming will proceed in the decades to come. One of the things that different climate models agree on is the energized state of the hydrologic cycle as the earth warms.

While climate models are unable to simulate small-scale weather events like thunderstorms, we can draw conclusions about what an energized hydrologic cycle might bring. Downpours from thunderstorms, such as that which caused the Shadyside, Ohio, flooding described in chapter 2, could become heavier, on average. Imagine a typical thunderstorm of the future, occurring somewhere over the Iowa countryside in the year 2075. On a warm, humid summer afternoon, giant thunderstorm clouds billow into the sky. Lightning crackles across the green farmland as the sky darkens. Southerly winds carry water vapor up into the bottom of the thunderstorms, feeding the storms with humidity. Much of the water vapor in the air probably comes from the Gulf of Mexico, many hundreds of miles to the south. As the water vapor rises, it becomes countless billions of cloud droplets and ice crystals, which together help form the raindrops that splash down on the countryside below.

So far, we've described a typical Iowa thunderstorm as it might exist today. In the future, however, if global warming proceeds as some scientists predict, the air will be more humid than it is today. The average rate of evaporation from the Gulf of Mexico will be higher than it is now. This humidity would be blown northward into the central United States and fed into thunderstorms, such as those which we imagine over Iowa in the year 2075. These

Future thunderstorms may intensify because of greater humidity resulting from increased water evaporation.

future summertime storms would become wetter as a result.

How much wetter is difficult to predict. A storm that drops five inches of rain today might drop six and a half inches in the latter

While storms might get wetter as a result of global warming, other factors, such as wind speed, also affect the weather and make it hard to accurately predict how it will act under different conditions.

half of the twenty-first century. It depends not only on the increased evaporation rate and water vapor content of the atmosphere, but also on other factors. Storms marching eastward across Iowa in advance of a fast-moving cold front would be no more likely to cause flooding than they would today because they would be moving too quickly to drop excessive rain in any given location. On the other hand, wetter, slow-moving thunderstorms might be able to cause flash flooding more quickly than they currently do.

With river flooding, however, the situation is even more complex. Floods aren't produced only by an excessive amount of water vapor in the air. The weather is an intricate chain of cause and effect, with numerous factors that can affect the outcome of any given event. For a river to flood, there must be much above-average precipitation over a relatively wide area for a long period of time—weeks or months. This requires not just an isolated cloudburst, but a persistent weather pattern that carries rain-bearing storms over the same area repeatedly. And while it's possible to say that global warming may raise evaporation rates and boost humidity levels, it's another matter to predict how global warming might affect overall weather patterns. We've seen that flooding can be linked to the oceans, in particular to El Niño and La Niña events. Scientists are unsure how changes in ocean water temperatures affect weather patterns, and they are even less sure how this relationship may change if global warming proceeds as many predict.

More certainty lies in the prospects for storm surge flooding in the future. As the planet warms, ocean levels will rise. There are two main reasons for this. The first is that a warmer atmosphere will melt land-based ice caps and glaciers, and their water will flow into the sea. Already, NASA scientists report that the ice cap over Greenland is shrinking at the rate of three feet per year around its edges. And photographs from satellites clearly show crumbling ice sheets over parts of Antarctica, with enormous icebergs breaking off and floating away into the ocean. The second reason that ocean levels will rise is a phenomenon called thermal expansion. When water warms, the water molecules move around faster. They collide and bounce off one another with greater energy, thereby creating

Satellite photos give us insight into other changing weather conditions worldwide, including the shrinkage of the Antarctic ice sheets, which many scientists attribute to global warming.

more space around themselves, on average. In effect, the water molecules expand outward from one another, increasing the overall volume of water. The ocean warms and expands, and water levels rise.

Current predictions for ocean rise are anywhere from five and a half to as much as thirty-two inches. The higher end of these estimates could have dire consequences for low-lying coastal regions. While thirty inches of ocean water rise would not be enough to flood most coastal cities outright, it would mean that there would be that much more water in storm-driven surges. Hurricanes and coastal winter storms would cause even greater damage as higher storm surges flooded more land. In fact, some research shows that the number of people threatened by storm surge would increase from 46 million today to perhaps over 100 million by the year 2100 if global warming continues its current trend.

At particular risk are the small island nations of the Indian, Atlantic, and Pacific Oceans. Many of these tropical islands are no more than five or ten feet above sea level. In the most extreme cases, an ocean level rise of thirty inches could put an entire island underwater. In other cases, rising ocean levels could flood the islands' natural underground drinking water supplies with salt water.

Which small town will become the next Shadyside, Ohio? What river will be the next to burst its banks as it fills with melting snow, like the Red River did in 1997? What stretch of coastline will be the next to become swamped by storm-driven ocean water? It's impossible to say. Global warming, however, hints that such events may become more severe and more frequent in the future. The prospects for river flooding are most unclear, while it's easier to link a warmer atmosphere with the kinds of isolated cloudbursts that produce flash floods. Storm surge flooding seems most likely to worsen in the decades to come. Whether from the ocean or from the sky, whether from rain or melting snow, flooding is yet one more potential threat posed by our changing climate.

Conclusion

There is little controversy about whether the earth is warming. Most of the debate about global warming centers around the questions of whether it will continue at its current pace in the future and what the effects of changing climate will be. One possible consequence of a warming planet is an energized hydrologic cycle. With warmer air and ocean temperatures, the average rate of evaporation will increase on a global scale. This will pump more water vapor into the atmosphere. The more water vapor in the air, the more water that's available for clouds, rain, and snow. Increase evaporation, and you increase precipitation. Increase precipitation, and you end up with more frequent and severe floods.

There's still much uncertainty, however. The atmosphere is a complex natural system, with shades of detail that evade the best modern computerized predictions. Climate models, the simulations of the atmosphere that scientists use to predict future weather, are good at painting with broad strokes. They can estimate overall trends and large-scale patterns. They can show how ocean levels will rise, raising the threat for storm surge flooding. They can show how a warmer world may be wetter, at least in certain parts of the globe. But climate models, the most advanced tools we have for predicting the future of global warming, cannot draw in the details. They are unable to simulate individual thunderstorms of the kind that can produce a surprise flash flood. They don't do a good job at showing

While scientific techniques, such as the use of climate models, can help us predict general weather trends, they cannot predict the specific natural disasters that still plague humanity.

how the oceans interact with the kinds of weather patterns that can lead to devastating river flooding.

The potential definitely exists for water to run wild on the earth in ways it hasn't before. With global warming, we're entering into a new relationship with the atmosphere. Perhaps the best way to respond to a flooding threat is to prepare now. People should not only review flooding safety tips, but think twice about building in river flood plains or along the beach. Global warming or not, floods will always be a threat in the future.

Glossary

climate The average weather conditions over a long period of time, generally decades or more.

climate model A computerized simulation of the atmosphere, used by scientists to predict changes in climate over long periods of time.

condensation The process whereby invisible, gaseous water vapor changes into liquid water.

El Niño A warming of tropical ocean water to above-average levels in the eastern Pacific Ocean.

evaporation   The process whereby liquid water changes into invisible, gaseous water vapor.

flash flood   A sudden overflow of a body of water; often occurs in streams and creeks when thunderstorms drop very heavy rain in a short period of time.

fossil fuel   Any fuel made from the decayed remains of ancient plant life; includes coal, natural gas, and oil. Fossil fuels take millions of years to create.

global warming   The warming of the planet due to increasing amounts of greenhouse gases in the atmosphere.

greenhouse effect   The natural warming effect that the atmosphere has on the earth; arises from the exchange of radiation between the air and the ground.

greenhouse gas   Any gas that efficiently absorbs outgoing radiation from the earth. The main greenhouse gases are water vapor, carbon dioxide, methane, nitrous oxide, chlorofluorocarbons, and ozone.

humidity A measure of the amount of water vapor in the air.

hydrologic cycle The transfer of water in gaseous, liquid, and solid forms between the atmosphere, the earth, and the oceans.

La Niña A cooling of ocean water to below-average levels in the tropical eastern Pacific.

precipitation Snow, rain, or anything else that forms inside a cloud and falls to the ground.

radiation Energy in the form of invisible electromagnetic waves that travel at the speed of light. Different kinds of radiation are characterized by wavelength, which is the distance from the crest of one wave to the next.

river flood The overflow of water from the banks of a river; usually occurs slowly, resulting from heavy rainfall over a long period of time.

runoff   The gravity-driven flow of water on land from high elevation to low elevation and eventually into the oceans.

storm surge   The rise in ocean water that results when wind piles up water against a coastline.

thermal expansion   The rise in ocean water resulting from warmer ocean temperatures.

transpiration   The process by which plants release some of their stored water into the air through pores on the undersides of their leaves.

water vapor   The invisible, gaseous form of water.

For More Information

Environmental Protection Agency (EPA)
Ariel Rios Building
1200 Pennsylvania Avenue NW
Washington, DC 20460-0003
(202) 260-2090
Web site: http://www.epa.gov/
     globalwarming
The EPA's global warming Web site is a good source for general information on our changing climate.

Federal Emergency Management Agency
500 C Street SW
Washington, DC 20472

(202) 646-4600
Web site: http://www.fema.gov
Includes information on floods and other kinds of disasters, and how to prepare for them.

National Climatic Data Center (NCDC)
Federal Building
151 Patton Avenue
Asheville, NC 28801-5001
(828) 271-4800
Web site: http://www.ncdc.noaa.gov
The NCDC Web site contains interesting information on precipitation records and major flooding events of the last twenty years.

Weatherwise Magazine
Heldref Publications
1319 18th Street NW
Washington, DC 20036-1802
Web site: http://www.weatherwise.org
A popular magazine about all things weather. Find it at your local library or newsstand.

For Further Reading

Allaby, Michael. *Floods* (Dangerous Weather Series). New York: Facts on File, 1997.

Eden, Philip, and Clint Twist. *Weather Facts.* New York: Dorling Kindersley, 1995.

Lauber, Patricia. *Flood: Wrestling with the Mississippi.* Washington, DC: National Geographic Society, 1996.

Newson, Lesley. *Devastation! The World's Worst Natural Disasters.* New York: Dorling Kindersley, 1998.

Sayre, April Pulley. *El Niño and La Niña: Weather in the Headlines.* Brookfield, CT: Twenty-First Century Books, 2000.

Stevens, William K. *The Change in the Weather: People, Weather, and the Science of Climate.* New York: Delacorte Press, 1999.

Suplee, Curt. "El Niño/La Niña." *National Geographic,* March 1999, pp. 72–95.

Williams, Jack. *The Weather Book.* 2nd edition. New York: Vintage Books, 1997.

Index

About the Author

Paul Stein has a B. S. in meteorology from Pennsylvania State University. He has eight years' experience as a weather forecaster, most recently as a senior meteorologist for the Weather Channel. Currently he develops computer systems and software that display and process weather-related data.

Photo Credits

Cover images © AP/Worldwide: flood waters in Elba, AL.

Cover inset © Robert Brakenridge, Dartmouth Flood Observatory:
      floods in Southeast Asia.

Front and back matter © Weatherstock: lightning storm.

Introduction background © Weatherstock: rainstorm.

Chapter 1 background © Digital Vision: ocean condensation.

Chapter 2 background © Weatherstock: lightning in Arizona.

Chapter 3 background © AP/Worldwide: flooding in Fort Collins, CO.

Chapter 4 background © Weatherstock: cumulous clouds.

Pp. 7, 8, 25, 28, 34, 53 © AP/Worldwide; pp. 12, 18, 24 © Corbis; p. 14 © Digital Vision; p. 15 © SP Parker/Photo Researchers, Inc.; pp. 17, 37, 47, 48 © Weatherstock; p. 22 © *The Gleaner*, AP/Worldwide; p. 27 © Marit Jentoft-Nilsen, NASA GSFC Visualization Analysis Lab; p. 38 © FPG International; p. 40 NASA Visible Earth; p. 44 © Billings Gazette/AP Worldwide; p. 46 © National Snow and Ice Data Center; p. 50 © Brian Montgomery, NASA GSFC.

Series Design and Layout

Geri Giordano